RAISE A BANNER TO THE LORD

60 Dynamic Banner Designs for Worship Settings

by Dale A. Bargmann

CPH®
SAINT LOUIS

To Jim, Jennie, and Barbara for their patience and support, and to my friends at Our Father for allowing me freedom of expression.

5 6 7 8 9 10 11 12   07 06 05 04 03 02 01

Contents

In Worship

Psalm 95:6

Banner 1

Preface

"It was he who gave some to be apostles, . . . some to be evangelists, and some to be pastors and teachers, to prepare God's people for works of service, so that the body of Christ may be built up" (Eph. 4:11–12).

How often have you left a worship service humming a hymn refrain or feeling the need for a further discussion of the ideas expressed in a sermon? No doubt, many times. But can you recall the times visual images have stirred your imagination? I venture to say, not as often.

Well-designed and crafted banners can convey the Gospel message as effectively and memorably as music and the spoken and written word. Of all the visual forms of art used in the church, banners are the most versatile. Stained-glass windows inspire awe and lend reality to the glory of God, but they cannot be moved or changed. Banners can be designed for special needs to give continuity to themes or emphasize sermon texts. They lend beauty and life to worship, and they are one means by which we can utilize our artistic talents to build up the body of Christ. Banners reinforce the message of the Gospel, and by so doing elevate the spirit, provoke thought, and incite action. As visual hymns of praise, banners summon our alleluias, calling out, as did the Psalmist, "Let everything that has breath praise the LORD" (Ps. 150:6).

Many of the designs in this book are outgrowths of worship experiences. While singing a hymn, reading a lesson, or listening to a choral piece or sermon, images began flowing through my imagination and, with pencil and paper in hand, I then attempted to transform them from my mind's eye into visual reality. That process has sometimes been frustrating, but more often than not it has been extremely rewarding. The greatest joy for me has come not from hanging one of my creations but from hearing the reactions of others to it. If my work provokes thought or makes a visual contribution to worship, then the struggle has been worthwhile.

I can only hope that you will also have a share of this joy by using some of the designs in this book to raise your own banners to the Lord.

Gathering Necessary Items

Design Notebook: It is a good idea to have a loose-leaf binder with filler paper handy at all times, to keep procedural notes, lists of supplies, fabric swatches, color ideas, and copies of banner designs for reference.

CONSTRUCTION TOOLS AND MATERIALS

Most of the tools and materials needed for constructing the designs in this book are listed below. They are not all necessary for any one design. At the beginning of a banner project, check the instructions first before deciding what to buy.

Cutting Tools

• Scissors—two pairs: one for paper, one reserved for cloth (paper dulls cutting edges).

• X-Acto knife and blades.

Marking Tools

• No. 2 pencils or .7 mm automatic pencils with HB black leads.

• Medium ballpoint pens—black and blue.

• Eagle Prismapastel pencils or Crayola colored pencils in light and dark colors for marking fabric—obtained through craft or art suppliers.

• Wooden stick (¾" × ¾" × 3") to serve as a makeshift compass for drawing large circles and arcs. For a pivot, drill a ¼" hole near one end and insert a pencil, eraser end down. Use a small C-clamp to secure another pencil, point down, to the other end. The C-clamp allows for adjustment to any needed radius.

• Circle templates, small compass, or French curves—aids for drawing curves and circles. Obtained through hobby, art, or drafting suppliers.

Paper for Patterns

• Tissue gift-wrapping paper (similar in weight to that used for dressmaker's patterns).

• Brown wrapping paper.

• Newspaper, especially the classified ads.

• Wide rolls of wrapping paper, particularly those with the pattern printed only on one side.

Bonding Materials

• Scotch Magic tape (green package).

• Scotch removable tape (blue package), or Scotch Safe Release masking tape.

• Double-stick tape.

• Masking tape.

• Elmer's Glue-All—general purpose white glue, best with cotton and cotton blends.

• Slomon's Sobo Glue, Aleene's Tacky Glue— white craft glues suitable for fabrics.

• Pellon Wonder-Under, Aleene's Fusible Web, and Therm O Web Heat-n-Bond—iron-on adhesives with paper backing: 17" wide; purchased in bulk, or prepackaged from cloth suppliers.

• Stitch Witchery— ¾" wide iron-on bonding web for linings and hems.

• Glue sticks.

• Velcro hook and loop strips, and Velcro adhesive (1 oz. tube)—for bonding.

Miscellaneous

- Plastic fishing-tackle box—for storing tools and small supplies.
- Opaque projector or overhead transparency projector.
- Ball-head straight pins.
- Lightweight pressing cloth—for protecting fabrics from direct contact with iron (a piece of 100% cotton muslin, a cotton dish towel, or an old bedsheet).
- Carpenter's square—L-shaped with 18" and 24" sides, or a large T-square.
- Yardstick.
- 12' retractable tape measure.
- 12" rule—preferably clear plastic.
- Iron and ironing board.
- Sewing machine and sewing needle with a selection of threads in colors to match fabrics being used.
- Wright's bias tape, double or single fold—for finishing raw fabric edges.
- Inexpensive paint brushes—1/2" and 1 1/2".

Hanging Supplies

- Hammer, screwdriver, and pliers.
- Drill, electric or push type, with bits.
- 4d smooth box nails, or similar.
- S- or 8-hooks (so named because of their shape).
- 3/4" dowels—lengths as needed.
- Lock seam or adjustable spring-pressure curtain rods, purchased at cloth or decorating suppliers.

  (All the above items are available through hardware suppliers.)
- Drapery weights.
- Fishing line—15 lb., or higher, test.

Special Purpose Materials

- For outlining: Crayola washable markers (purchased from craft suppliers); permanent felt-tip markers (regular tip, in black, and other colors as needed); fluorescent highlighters; yarns (4 ply, 100% acrylic); embroidery paints (preferably the puff type in various colors); washable markers (Crayola or Kodak, purchased in sets from school or craft suppliers).
- Acrylic paints, 2 fl. oz. tubes, Liquitex, Hyplar, or Windsor Newton brand—from art or hobby suppliers.
- Spray paint (12 oz. can) or a can of quick-drying enamel, preferably red.

Fabric Choices

Pick a fabric supplier with a large selection. There are many attractive fabrics suitable for making banners, but some types work better than others. Generally speaking, 100% cottons and cotton blends work best. Avoid stretchy knits (especially 100% polyesters) and those with loose weaves or heavy textures.

Recommended Fabrics

Broadcloth—100% cotton or polyester-cotton blend; 45" wide; relatively inexpensive; excellent color range, but lighter shades do not cover as well as darker ones.

Felt—100% acrylic or polyester (some suppliers may stock 100% wool, but it is not as readily available); 72" wide; smooth surface; good color range and intensity; good as a background material: it is economical, readily available, nonfraying, and does not require lining (although lining does add stability).

Flannel —100% cotton (avoid polyester); 45" wide; limited number of solid colors available; easy to glue; accepts paint well (see "Learning Useful Techniques").

Interlock knits—polyester-cotton or polyester-rayon blend; 60" wide; nonfraying; good color range.

Muslin—100% cotton; 45"–108" wide; primarily

available in white and natural unbleached, also in a number of solid colors; light in weight with a smooth finish; covers well and works well with paints and markers.

Poly-cotton sheeting—100% cotton; 45" wide; heavier and more opaque than broadcloth; good color range, although not as extensive as broadcloth.

Poplin—cotton-polyester blend; 45" wide; heavier and more opaque than broadcloth; good for backgrounds, if lined.

Robe velour—60" wide; 80% acetate/20% nylon; gives a plush look similar to velvet, but without the weight; nonfraying; good for lettering on selected designs.

Trigger cloth—60" wide; available only in black, white, and basic colors; a good background material on selected designs because of its weight and smooth texture; needs to be lined.

Do not be afraid to mix materials. Plan to use heavier fabrics (felt, poplin, trigger cloth) for backgrounds and lighter fabrics (flannel, broadcloth) for design elements. Also try drapery and upholstery fabrics for backgrounds, but avoid those with heavy or rough textures, or all-over patterns.

Specialty Fabrics

Lycra—60% Lycra/40% nylon; relatively expensive; available in several good bright colors, including fluorescents.

Solid taffeta—100% polyester; 60" wide; good for processional banners.

Tissue lamé—100% polyester; 60" wide; good for simulating metals: gold, silver, copper; thin and unravels easily, but both problems can be fixed by using a fusible web for bonding.

Lining Materials

Drapery lining—48" wide; poly-cotton blend.

Fusible interfacing—22" and 45" widths.

Sale and remnant tables are a good source of heavy fabrics to use for linings. Extra-wide drapery and upholstery materials, *suitable for backing large banners, can often be found at reduced prices as well.*

FULL-SIZE DESIGNS

Enlarging the Designs

Pattern Method

The best way to enlarge designs is to use an opaque projector. This allows the image to be cast directly from the page in the book. Next best is to use an overhead transparency projector, most likely available from the church office. Its biggest advantage is that the design can be scaled to a size that fits the dimensions of the display area. To use an overhead projector, first use a copier to transfer the design in the book to a clear acetate sheet.

1. Project the design onto a smooth wall at eye level. Adjust the image to the desired size by moving the projector toward or away from the wall, measuring with a 12' rule. Turn the projector off.

2. Prepare the sheet of paper that will serve as the full-size pattern by cutting it to the exact size of the finished banner. Make sure all sides are square. This is an important step if the finished banner is to hang properly, because the pattern will be used both for cutting the design pieces and for sizing the background.

3. Turn on the projector and tape the blank pattern paper to the wall within the image area. Use removable tape to prevent wall damage. *Make sure the image is square with the paper.*

4. Trace the design lines in pencil (a marker can bleed through the paper) taking special care with the lettering. Keep a rule handy for straight lines, and a compass, French curve, or circle template for curves.

5. Block the projected image in sections to check for missed lines. Look carefully at the lettering again and make sure that the lines are plumb with each other.

6. Turn off the projector, and, before removing the pattern from the wall, do a final check for any untraced elements.

7. To aid reassembly after cutting, number each of the shapes and indicate its color. Transfer the numbers to the corresponding shapes on the

original in the book. Also, to prevent pieces from being accidently placed upside down, indicate the top of each with a *T*.

8. Set the pattern aside. Do not cut it apart yet. It needs to be kept whole for some of the next steps.

Have a second sheet of paper handy as some of the designs contain overlapping design elements that require separate tracings.

No Pattern Method

For simple designs with few overlapping elements, consider projecting the design directly onto the cloth pieces, skipping the paper pattern altogether.

1. Project the design directly onto a wall.

2. Use a 12' tape measure to size the image to the exact size of the finished banner.

3. Attach the cloth pieces to the wall over the image area with safe-release masking tape.

4. Trace the design areas with clearly contrasting pastel pencils or colored pencils onto the fabrics for the banner.

5. Cut out the pieces just inside the pencil lines as the lines might otherwise show on the finished banner.

Estimating Fabric Needs

Background—to determine the amount of background material needed, start with the dimensions of the finished banner. Then:

• add 2" to the *length* to compensate for cutting error, plus 3" for each hem.

• add 2" to the *width* to compensate for cutting error, plus 2" for hems or sewn-in linings (not necessary if lining with fusible interfacing or other materials bonded with Stitch Witchery).

• add another 2" to both *length* and *width* to compensate for shrinkage from prewashing (not necessary for upholstery fabrics or felt, which do not require preshrinking).

• add extra yardage to allow for experimentation with unfamiliar materials and processes.

Lining—Purchase enough to cover the background piece plus a little extra.

Fabrics for design elements—use the full-size pattern to make rough measurements of lettering and color areas. Do not scrimp. Allow for error and experimentation. These measurements will also determine the amount of iron-on adhesive to purchase, if it is being used to attach the design pieces to the background.

When making estimates, remember that most fabrics, with the exception of those noted above, are manufactured in 45" widths.

Putting the Banner Together

PREPARATIONS

For assembly, it is best to work in a well-lit area on a table large enough to handle the full-size banner. It is also possible to use a carpeted floor, or any space, where the banner can be left undisturbed until completed.

To prevent puckering and uneven bonding, fabrics (except felt and upholstery materials) must be preshrunk and pressed smooth. Preshrinking is especially important for 100% cotton and cotton blends because it removes the sizing or starch that can interfere with bonding. Preshrink the fabrics by putting them through a complete wash and dry cycle. Be sure to check fabric care instructions at the time of purchase. As with regular laundering, light and dark fabrics need to be separated.

Background

Materials

• Carpenter's square, or T-square

• 12" rule

- Pastel pencils, or Crayola colored pencils (light or dark, to contrast with fabric color)
- Straight pins
- Sharp cloth scissors

Procedure

1. Lay background cloth *wrong* side up on the work surface and place the carefully squared pattern on top.

2. Align pattern edges with the fabric weave and secure with several straight pins.

3. Use the pattern to measure cutting lines, with allowances for finishing. Add 2 1/2"–3" to the length for each pole loop. Add less to the bottom if using drapery weights. If the lining is to be sewn to the back, add 1" to the width for seams. Disregard if the sides are to be left as cut edges (as on felt), or if the lining is to be bonded to the back.

4. Apply fray-check along the cutting lines to prevent edges from unraveling after cutting (unnecessary with felt).

Design Pieces

The pattern pieces need to be cut out. Stack them, as work proceeds, according to the color fabric they will be used on later. Set the larger background pieces aside for use as positioning templates during the process of final assembly.

Before tracing the pattern pieces onto their respective fabrics, a method for attaching the fabric design pieces to the background of the banner needs to be determined.

The least expensive method is gluing. White glue is easiest to use with fabrics. Of the ordinary brands on the market, the best is Elmer's Glue-All. It is heavy enough in consistency not to soak in too quickly; its applicator tip delivers a smooth, even flow; and it has demonstrated its capacity to hold banners together even through years of continuous use.

Also suitable for fabrics, though more expensive, are craft glues such as Slomon's Sobo Glue and Aleene's Tacky Glue. All dry clear but have several disadvantages. They can cause moisture-sensitive fabrics to pucker if not preshrunk first; they can bleed through thinner fabrics, leaving a shiny discoloration; and they do not work well with polyester.

An alternative to gluing is the use of highly-recommended iron-on adhesives like Pellon Wonder-Under, Aleene's Fusible Web, or Therm O Web Heat-n-Bond. They can be purchased in both prepackaged amounts or off the bolt by the yard. Though somewhat more expensive than gluing, they bring several advantages to the banner-making process. They

- are easier and faster to use than glue.
- leave no mess.
- eliminate frayed edges.
- can be applied in any direction.
- can be dry cleaned or washed.
- are good for fabrics that react adversely to moisture.
- are good with fabrics that do not take glue.

Testing, as always, is the best way to decide on a method. Use 6" swatches of the materials involved. Try gluing pieces of broadcloth, flannel, and polycotton sheeting to felt (use Elmer's and a craft glue). Make one piece a letter like *S* or *E*. Then bond the same fabrics with squares of fusible web, following the instructions furnished with the material. Allow the samples to cool and dry completely. Be sure, in all cases, to time the procedure. Then compare results:

- Check the edges for fraying and puckering.
- Check for adhesive bleed-through.
- Check to see that the pieces lie flat.
- Check the strength of the bond by trying to pull the pieces apart.

All things considered, the iron-on adhesive usually proves the best. It is more expensive, but this disadvantage seems minor when compared with the time it saves.

ASSEMBLY

To Begin

1. Press the background to remove wrinkles.
2. For reference, mark seam and hem

allowances with straight pins placed parallel to the edges and spaced about 12" apart.

3. Position reserved pattern templates and secure with straight pins.

Gluing Method

Materials

- Paper pattern pieces
- Fabrics for design pieces
- Straight pins
- Sharp cloth scissors
- Carpenter's square
- Glues

Procedure

1. Lay all fabrics for the design pieces *right* side up. Position pattern pieces, also *right* side up, on top. Leave about 1/4" between each piece to be cut. *Align all the letters in the same direction*, that is, on the same grain. Secure all the pattern pieces with straight pins.

2. Cut pieces out using smooth strokes to avoid ragged edges. Check the original design in the book for any abutting elements and cut one 1/4" larger so that it will fit under the other. Arrange the pieces roughly in position on the background as they are cut.

3. Remove the pins and arrange the pieces in final position. Step back and check for reversed letters and awkward spacing.

4. Prepare for gluing. If the design has overlapping elements, the lower elements need to be attached first. Temporarily set the upper ones aside.

5. Take one element at a time and lay the arm of the carpenter's square across the center of the element to hold it in position. Lift the exposed half of the element away from the background and apply a steady, unbroken line of glue along all edges of its underside. Drop it back into position and press down gently. Repeat with the other shapes until half of each is glued. Let them dry thoroughly, and then glue the other halves using the same method.

6. Reposition any pieces that had to be set aside and repeat the gluing procedure.

7. Allow everything to dry completely

before handling further.

Do not discard letter patterns. Put them in large clasp envelopes, record the contents of the envelope on the outside of the envelope, and file the envelope for future projects.

Iron-on Adhesive Method

Materials

- Fabrics for design pieces
- Fusible adhesive to cover
- Straight pins
- Sharp cloth scissors
- Iron and ironing board

Read the instructions that come with the fusible interfacing carefully, and do a test on swatches of the fabrics for each banner.

Procedure

1. Preheat the iron on the dry wool setting (do not use steam).

2. The fabric for the design pieces goes *face down* on the ironing board. Position an adhesive sheet textured side down on top of the fabric.

3. Place the iron on the paper side of the adhesive sheet and press 1–3 seconds *only*. (The object is not to melt the glue, but to transfer it to the back of the fabric.) Let cool.

4. Pin paper pattern pieces *right side* up to the front (cloth side) of the prepared fabrics. It is especially important that letters be aligned in the same direction, that is, on the same grain.

5. Cut the design pieces from the prepared fabric according to the pattern. Remove the pins. Carefully peel off the paper backing and position, adhesive side down, on the background. Use reserved pattern templates as guides.

6. Double-check wording for spelling and reversed or upside down letters. Also check spacing and alignment.

7. Preheat the iron on dry wool setting.

8. Cover an area with a damp pressing cloth and press approximately 10 seconds. Do not slide the iron back and forth. Lift it to the next position, overlapping iron placement to

insure complete bonding. *Do not overheat.* (Overheating causes adhesive to migrate back toward the iron.) For large areas, begin fusing in the center and work outward to the sides and corners.

While bonding the design elements, move the banner as little as possible to prevent jostling the arrangement. Place the ironing board adjacent to and level with the work surface and slide the banner onto it for fusing. A sheet of corrugated cardboard also makes a suitable ironing surface if the work surface is the floor. Simply slide the sheet of cardboard under the area to be fused.

FINISHING

Lining

Lining is recommended for practically all banners because it gives added stability when hanging. It is optional for banners with backgrounds of felt and necessary for banners with backgrounds of woven or lightweight fabrics.

Preshrink lining materials, except felt, upholstery, and drapery fabrics by machine washing or pressing with an iron and a wet pressing cloth. To prepare fusible interfacing, dip it in a sink of warm water, lay it flat between bath towels and pat it dry to remove excess moisture. Hang it to air dry.

Method I. Apply a fusible interfacing to the back. Primarily for lightweight fabrics; also poplins, linens, wools, and fabrics with special finishes.

1. Trim the banner to its finished size, allowing an extra 3" at the top for a pole casing. No allowances are needed for the sides or bottom.

2. Place the banner *face side down* on the work surface. Position the interfacing *rough (adhesive) side down* on top of it. Pin it in place along the edges.

3. Preheat the iron on the wool setting. Baste at a few points along the edges by pressing lightly with the tip of the iron. Remove the pins.

4. Cover the interfacing with a damp pressing cloth and fuse about 15 seconds. Do not slide the iron. Fuse section by section, overlapping the previous area. Let cool.

5. Turn the banner over and repeat the ironing process to achieve a secure bond.

6. Trim any excess lining material.

Method II. Bond a heavy fabric to the back. Primarily for felt and heavier background fabrics.

1. Trim the banner to its finished size, allow 2 1/2"–3" at the top for a pole casing. No allowances are needed for the sides or bottom.

2. Cut the lining material slightly larger than the banner. Place it wrong side up on the work surface. Position the banner *face side up* on top of it.

3. Preheat the iron at the wool setting.

4. Place strips of Stitch Witchery between the fabric layers along the edges of the banner.

5. Cover with a damp pressing cloth and press along the edges for 10 seconds. *Do not slide the iron.*

6. Turn the banner over and press along the edges for another 10 seconds.

7. Turn the banner over once more and trim any excess lining material.

With either of these methods, the fused edges will, with careful handling, not unravel. However, they can be dressed up with strips of quilt edging in a color to match the background.

Method III. Stabilize edges before lining. For fabrics that unravel easily.

1. Trim the banner to its finished size, allowing 3" at the top for a pole casing, and allowing 1" at the bottom and each side.

2. Turn the banner *face side down.*

3. Fold the side and bottom edges over, forming 1" hems. Press with the iron to crease and bond to the back of the banner with strips of Stitch Witchery.

4. Cut a lining of heavy cloth slightly smaller than the finished banner and bond it to the background along all the edges with Stitch Witchery.

Method IV. Sew a heavy fabric or drapery lining to the back. An alternate method for felt, and medium and heavyweight fabrics.

1. Trim the banner to its finished size, adding 3" to the top for a pole casing, and adding 5/8" to each side and the bottom.

2. Place the lining material *right side up* on the work surface. Place the banner *right side down* on top of it making sure that the grains of the fabrics are aligned.

3. Pin the side and bottom edges together.

4. Set the sewing machine to "straight stretch stitch." Sew the sides and bottom together with a 5/8" seam leaving the top end open just like a pillow case.

5. Trim the seams and cut the bottom corners off at a 45º angle.

6. Turn the banner and lining *right side out*.

7. Sew or bond the top edges together.

Finishing the Top Edge

The designs in this book work best when hung by inserting a pole through a simple 3" casing applied at the top. No matter which lining method has been used, all banners can be finished at the top in the same way.

Procedure

1. Turn the banner *face side down*.

2. Mark a line 6" down from and parallel to the top edge. Fold the top over to meet the line, forming a 3" casing. Bond with Stitch Witchery.

3. For added security, edge stitch the casing with needle and thread using a simple whipstitch.

All methods provide enough stability so that a bottom pole is unnecessary. If the bottom edge should curl or sag, add drapery weights to the lower corners as appropriate.

Outlining Design Elements

Before any banner is hung, it should be thoughtfully appraised from a distance. If the images fail to stand out, or are unclear, simple outlining of one or two of the design elements can be used to bring things into focus.

Fluorescent highlighters (1/4" wide) add subtle radiance without becoming obtrusive.

The best colors are hot pink, yellow, orange, chartreuse, and light blue. Draw lines about 3/16" wide directly on the background, or on the edge of the elements. Make samples of both to see which works better.

Permanent felt-tip markers (1/4" tip) in colors contrasting with both the background and the elements being outlined will sharpen definition considerably. For instance, outline a white form set against a dark blue background with an orange marker, or outline a chartreuse form set against a yellow background with a dark green marker. Draw the lines 1/8"–1/4" wide on the edge of the forms. This technique works best on 100% cottons or cotton blends with a smooth finish.

Yarns (4-ply, 100% acrylic) add the extra dimension of depth and anchor the elements in place. The process can be time consuming, but the results are well worth it. Remember:

• Yarn outlines are best applied after lining.

• Color combinations need to be tested by doing a dry outline first.

• Care should be taken when pressing. (Prolonged exposure to steam can soften the glue and cause the yarn to loosen.)

With these pointers in mind:

1. Slide a sheet of corrugated cardboard under the area to be outlined.

2. With sharp scissors, cut the end of the yarn square and dab it with a bit of glue to prevent unraveling.

3. Outline the shape with an even, unbroken line of white glue about the width of the yarn. Begin at a corner or point, if possible, and lay the yarn gently onto the glue line. Do not pull. Press it in with the fingers.

4. To bend the yarn around corners, secure it with vertical pins stuck down through the strands and into the cardboard.

5. Cut the finishing end of the yarn only after most of the outline is in place.

Fabric paints (puff type) are a good alternative to yarn, especially with fabrics that do not accept glue well. Work quickly to keep the lines uniform. Practice on scraps first. One undesirable quality of fabric paint is its semigloss finish when dry.

Washable markers are useful for shading and work well on fabrics that are 100% cotton or cotton blends with a smooth finish. Lightly outline the shape with a 1/4"–1/2" wide line, and then, with an inexpensive 1/2" watercolor brush, dampen the line and the area immediately around it with tap water. The marker will bleed, creating a subtle color gradation. Allow to dry naturally. For best results, use colors within the same family as that of the shape being outlined, for example, red on pink, violet on lavender, or dark green on chartreuse. A certain amount of daring is required for this procedure, but the results are worth it. Always do a test piece first.

Outlining adds a personal touch to a banner. Like the amen to a prayer, the alleluia at Easter, or the artist's signature on a painting, it signifies completion.

DISPLAY

Improper display can diminish the finished product. Consequently, significant attention should be given to the way in which banners are hung.

Where practical, banners should be hung 3"–6" away from the wall rather than flush with it. This lends depth and a feeling of life. All efforts should be made to keep hanging methods as unobtrusive as possible. Avoid heavy cords, ropes, or chains. One solution is to suspend the banners from above. Hang two lengths of clear fishing line from the sanctuary ceiling about 3' apart and 6" out from the wall. Tie S-hooks to each at the point where the top of the banner will be suspended. (Be sure the points are level with each other.) Drive small 4d box nails into the ends of a 3/4" dowel the width of the banner. Leave 1/2" of the nails exposed. Suspend the banner by slipping the nails through the S-hooks. Changing banners is relatively easy with a stepladder, and, because the lines are virtually invisible, they can be left in place when no banner is displayed.

Attached to the Building

Valance curtain rods provide a practical alternative for both seasonal and permanent wall displays. Lengths can be adjusted to fit banners ranging in width from 26"–82". They are supported by two small brackets, and, of major advantage, project 3"–5 1/2" (depending on brand) from the wall. Manufacturers include Gold Seal, Graber, and Newell. Adjustable spring pressure curtain rods can be utilized in the same way. They also come in variable lengths, ranging from 36"–60" to 48"–72".

As a Freestanding Element

If wall space is limited, build a freestanding pole. However, the caution implicit in this suggestion is that simple hanging from a cord allows the banner to swing or slide back and forth. This problem is solved by adding a rigid horizontal pole to the top of the stand (see illustration).

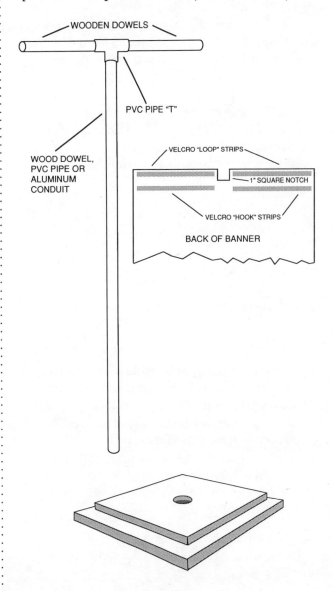

Procedure

1. All materials for the stand can be found at a building materials supplier. The vertical pole can be wood or metal. It should be at least a foot longer than the banners it is to support and long enough to enable a seated congregation to see the banner.

2. Look in the plumbing supplies for a PVC pipe T-fitting for the top end. It should fit so tightly that gluing is unnecessary. Simply jamb it onto one end of the pole and give it a few taps with a hammer.

3. For the crossbar, buy a wooden dowel the same diameter as the vertical pole, cut the dowel in half and jamb the halves into the openings of the T.

4. For a base, cut two squares of ³/₄" plywood, one 18" × 18" and one 12" × 12". Stack them and nail or screw them together. Drill a hole in the center of the diameter of the vertical pole.

5. To prepare the banner for hanging, cut a 1" square notch in the center of the top edge of the banner. With Velcro adhesive, attach Velcro loop strips to the back of the banner from the sides to the notch along the top edge. Then, attach hook strips 3" down from and parallel to the top edge. To hang, drape the banner over the top of the horizontal pole and mate the Velcro strips. This method is quite practical, especially for processional banners.

Banners are works of art created for the specific purposes of enhancing worship, encouraging activity, and glorifying God. They should not be seen as merely decorative adornments, to add a note of interest or a splash of color to otherwise drab surroundings. Nor should they be seen as elaborate craft projects. Bannermakers should be confident in their work. There is no need for added gimmicks such as fringe, tassels, or decorative ribbons. Such trims have a place on throw pillows, draperies, and other home projects. But, on banners, especially the designs in this book, they are unnecessary. Not only do they detract from the feeling of the designs, but they also, in practical terms, tend to loosen or unravel, creating a maintenance problem.

Learning Useful Techniques

LETTERING

Letterspacing

Proper spacing of individual letters in a word is vitally important to the overall appearance and readability of a banner. Inconsistent or cramped spacing makes the viewer more conscious of the letters than the words.

If every letter were rectangular, then spacing would be easy. It would merely be a matter of measuring equal distances between rectangles, as with this group:

HMN

But the variety in widths and shapes of individual letters makes this impossible. The only pure rectangles in the modern alphabet are HMN (previous column). Look what happens to this even spacing when curved or irregular forms are introduced:

NHAOCYTI

Everything seems out of place, especially the A and Y. As these examples demonstrate, letter spacing cannot be left to chance. Nor can it be determined by a rigid set of rules. It is done aesthetically, by eye, so that the spaces appear to be even. This is not as difficult as it sounds. The human eye is easily deceived.

Compare these two rectangles. Which is larger?

— I

To most people, the vertical one appears to be larger, but in actuality, both rectangles are the same size.

To space lettering correctly, imagine that the blank areas between letters are filled with water, and try as much as possible to equalize the area the eye must "swim" to read from letter to letter. When lettering is properly spaced, the amount of liquid between letters appears to be the same.

Spaced by eye, the lettering from above appears as follows:

NHAOCYTI

General Lettering Principles

The letters needing the most space between them are those made with single strokes, such as *i* and *l*. They need breathing room to keep from seeming squashed.

illi

Slightly less space is needed between rectangular letters, for instance, *M* and *N*.

MN

A medium space is needed between a rectangular letter and a rounded letter, for instance, *N* and *O*, or *n* and *d*.

NO   nd

Even less space is needed between two rounded letters, such as, *O* and *C*, or *b* and *o*.

OC   bo

The odd but frequent combinations such as

A and *T*, *V* and *Y*, or *L* and *T* can be virtually abutted, or even allowed to touch or overlap. Their distinctive shapes make them easy to distinguish.

AT VY LT

With letter spacing, there is actually only one absolute: set rules aside and trust the eye. Beginners usually space the letters too widely, but with practice the spacing will become tighter.

Word Spacing

For banners, a good rule of thumb for determining the spacing of words is to use the width of an *N* as a starting point, keeping in mind that words, like letters, are spaced by eye and not by some arbitrary and regular measurement. It is possible to use narrower spacing if working area is limited, but the words should never be so tightly spaced that they blend into alphabet soup, nor so widely spaced that they lose their flow and readability. The only way to acquire this all important skill is to practice.

Letter Size

The word *Christ* below illustrates another important lettering principle.

Christ
Christ

When guidelines are added, as in the second example, it becomes apparent that the letter forms with curves are relatively larger. This is standard practice for all lettering, both typeset and hand drawn. It is yet another deception necessary to compensate for the perception of the human eye.

For example, compare these two shapes without measuring. Which is taller?

The rectangle appears taller to the eye, but measurement reveals that they are both the same height. Because of the way the eye perceives rounded shapes, letters like *C, G, J,* and *O* are always made slightly larger. On a banner, this can be ¼"–1", sometimes even more, depending on the banner scale. Applying this principle will make the same shapes appear more equal.

Line Spacing

In general, the minimum amount of space between lines of lettering is the amount needed so that the descenders (see Glossary) of the letters in the upper line will not become confused with the ascenders of the letters in the lower line.

All things proclaim the existence of God

Notice how the g in the top line interferes with the t in the bottom line. It is also difficult to read. Below, the same lines are shown properly spaced.

All things proclaim the existence of God

Capital letters, which have no ascenders or descenders, can be spaced quite closely and still be distinguished.

HE HAS MADE ALL THINGS NEW

A Short Glossary of Lettering Terms

- Ascenders—the parts of lowercase letters extending above the main body, for example, *b, d, h, k.*
- Baseline—the invisible guideline on which a line of lettering sits.
- Descenders—the parts of lowercase letters extending below the main body, for example, *g, j, p, q, y.*
- Lowercase—commonly known as small letters; so called because, in printing, these characters are kept in the lower cases or trays of type cabinets.
- Sans serif—a type style without serifs, for example, Aa Bb Cc Dd Ee Ff Gg Hh Ii
- Serif—the decoration on the end of a letter stroke, for example, Aa Bb Cc Dd Ee Ff Gg Hh Ii
- Uppercase—commonly known as capital letters; so-called because, in printing, these characters are kept in the upper cases or trays of type cabinets.

Lettering is an intricate and fascinating art. Keeping the principles of this section in mind makes it less difficult at first and easy later on.

Quick Lettering Patterns

Custom banners are often commissioned for weddings, anniversaries, or other special occasions where planning and construction time is limited. Most of that valuable time is often spent on patterns for the lettering. It would be easy if it were possible to paint the words directly on the background. But paint and cloth are not that compatible, and it is difficult to achieve a professional look by this method. There are other lettering techniques, however, that do yield professional results with minimal effort.

Hand-Lettering

Materials

- Sheets of newsprint
- Masking tape or glue stick
- 12 oz. can of spray paint (red is a good contrast to the black print on the paper) OR
- A pint can of quick-drying enamel and an inexpensive 1"–1 1/2" wide natural-bristle brush

Procedure

1. Glue or tape newspaper sheets together into one piece equal in size to the finished banner.

2. In a well-ventilated area (perhaps a garage) tack the paper sheet to the wall at eye level (or lay it on the floor). Keep extra sheets handy to allow for mistakes.

3. *With spray paint*: Hold can 3"–6" from the paper and write the words in order starting at the upper left. A cursive style with simplified strokes generally works best. After drying, the strokes can be refined with a felt-tip marker.

4. *With enamel and brush*: Use the best possible block lettering style and remember that mistakes are easily corrected during cutting.

5. Cut letters out and use like any other pattern.

The results of hand-lettering are spontaneous and personal.

Book Lettering

Materials

- A photocopier.
- An X-Acto knife or a pair of sharp scissors.
- A book on calligraphy, typography, or lettering that shows complete alphabets in different styles. (Section 745.6 of the local library should have a choice of such books.)

Procedure

1. Make copies of the desired styles of lettering and add them to the design notebook. Be sure to include all letters and examples of both upper and lowercase letters for each chosen alphabet. Bold styles work best. Look for sans serif typefaces such as: Futura Display, Avant Garde, or Franklin Gothic. Look for serif typefaces such as: Goudy Bold, or Garamond Bold. As an alternative, look for simulated handwriting: Kaufman Script, Brush Script.

2. When lettering is needed for a project, e.g., adding the names of the bride and bridegroom to a wedding banner, it is then easy to choose an appropriate style from among the alphabets already stored in the design notebook.

3. Set the photocopier to maximum enlargement percentage and copy the sample alphabet. Copy these enlargements successively until the letters are scaled to the needed size. It will take several steps, but it is quicker and more accurate than tracing by hand.

4. Carefully cut out the individual letters with an X-Acto knife or sharp scissors.

The results of book lettering will be stylish and consistent.

Computer-Generated Lettering

This technique saves a lot of tracing and increases accessibility to a variety of lettering styles.

Materials

- A computer
- A printer
- A photocopier

Procedure

1. Select the font and size of typeface (probably, as large as possible, depending upon the machine).

2. Type the words needed for the banner and print them out.

3. If necessary, enlarge the letters using the photocopier. Very large sizes may reproduce only one letter per sheet of paper.

Save toner by designating the font as an outline.

COMBINING COLORS

Choosing Colors

There are several ways to coordinate colors for a banner.

A color wheel can be useful, but it also carries the danger of turning what could be an artistic process into a merely mechanical one.

Another place to turn for ready-to-go color combinations is a fabric dealer. Pay particular attention to floral prints and other multicolored fabrics. Purchase narrow strips of the best of them. Add them to the design notebook and then borrow three or four colors from one of the swatches when other ideas do not seem to work.

The best place to look is the natural world, where the glories of God's creation appear in infinitely beautiful combinations. Sunrises reveal magentas, purples, peaches, reds, oranges, pinks, blues, and yellows. They give way to a sky filled with shades of blue, gray, and white. From there, turn to the purple and blue mountains, green trees with brown trunks, and flowers combining variegated greens with reds, yellows, oranges, violets, and pinks. Nature provides a color wheel to stir the imagination. Use a camera to capture especially striking color combinations and add them to the design notebook for ready reference.

Special Rainbow Technique

It is possible to create a stunning effect by literally painting the colors into the fabric of a banner. Use this technique, for instance, on the Baptism banner (banner 14) to turn the lettering in the lower part of the design (indicated in outline) into a rainbow.

Materials

- Empty 1–2 gallon plastic bucket

- 2 fl. oz. tubes of artist's acrylic paint in red, orange, yellow, green, blue, and violet

- An inexpensive 1"–1 1/2" wide natural-bristle brush

- 2 1/2 yds. 100% cotton flannel, prewashed

- Spray bottle for water

- A large, smooth, flat work area, ideally a concrete floor, or, a sheet of plywood

Procedure

1. Lay cloth on work surface and spray with warm water to dampen evenly.

2. Squeeze about 1/4 – 1/3 of the red acrylic paint into the bucket and, with the paint brush, stir while gradually adding about a pint of water; mix thoroughly. Though watery, the diluted color will retain surprising intensity.

3. To avoid unwanted blotches, rinse brush and squeeze dry.

4. Paint a 5"– 6" × 7' red stripe along one edge of the cloth, making sure the color is evenly spread.

5. Empty and rinse bucket.

6. Repeat steps 2 through 5 with, in succession, orange, yellow, green, blue, and violet. Slightly overlap the bands of color so they will blend naturally into each other. The six colored stripes should cover a 34"–36" wide area.

7. *Allow to dry flat.* Do not hang up in an attempt to lessen drying time. Gravity will pull color pigments downward, creating a muddy mess near the bottom.

8. Once thoroughly dry, the rainbow fabric can be treated like any other cloth. Lay it *face* side up on a flat surface. Arrange letter patterns *right* side up on top. It is important that they be aligned properly so the rainbow effect does not appear jumbled on the completed banner. Trace with a No. 2 pencil or a colored pencil.

9. If bonding with glue: cut out the letters, position carefully on the lower part of the banner and follow the gluing procedure in "Putting the Banner Together."

10. If bonding with an iron-on adhesive: fuse adhesive sheets to the back of the painted fabric and cut out the letters. *Test with scraps cut from the edges to be sure the paint does not interfere with the bonding process.* If satisfied with the results, proceed as directed in "Putting the Banner Together."

11. Any time an iron is used on this fabric, use a damp pressing cloth to protect the fabric. Otherwise the paint will scorch or leave a residue on the sole plate of the iron.

Somewhat the same effect can be achieved with 6" wide strips of cloth, one in each of the six colors. Use 1/2" wide strips of fusible web to bond them together into a single piece. (Either method will create an eye-catching effect, but, while somewhat messy, the painting technique is more spontaneous and personal.)

AN EXERCISE IN CREATIVITY

The main purpose of this exercise is to utilize the odd fabric scraps accumulated from other projects.

Materials

- Background fabric, preferably felt
- Fusible web, sufficient to cover background
- Boxes of saved fabric scraps
- Sharp scissors
- Assorted items necessary for finishing and hanging (pins, lining material, Stitch Witchery, etc.)

Procedure

1. Pick a size for the banner—2' × 8' or 3' × 6' are good proportions—and purchase background material in either dark blue or dark green (these colors provide a good contrast to most other colors).

2. Cut background to size, adding necessary hem and casing allowances. Place *face side up* on the work surface.

3. Pick a word theme. One of joy or praise is best. One that comes immediately to mind is *Let all creation sing.* The Psalms are a good place to go for inspiration, for example, "Sing to the LORD" (Psalm 147:7), or, "I will praise the LORD all my life" (Psalm 146:2). Lines from favorite hymns are also excellent, for example, "Joyful, joyful we adore thee" (*LBW* 551) or "Lift every voice and sing" (*LBW* 562).

4. For the lettering, use patterns saved from other projects from which to randomly select the letters needed (it does not matter if they are not the same style). Arrange them on the background to see how they work together. Or experiment with the quick lettering techniques described earlier.

5. Pick through the fabric scrap collection to find pieces and colors that stand out against the background.

6. Put fusible adhesive *paper side up* on a flat surface. Reverse the letter patterns and trace them with a pencil. Space them closely to minimize waste.

7. Cut out the letters and fuse them to the back of the fabric scraps. Let them cool, cut around the fused letters, and peel off the paper backing. Arrange the letters on the background material in a tightly spaced block roughly covering the upper two-thirds of the banner.

8. On the remainder of the adhesive sheet, sketch imaginative shapes inspired by nature (flowers, birds, trees, human figures, stars, wavy lines for water, swirls for clouds). Keep them simple and childlike. (This would be a good project for a Sunday school class.)

9. Cut out the shapes and, as with the letters, fuse them to the back of the randomly selected scraps. Let them cool and peel off the paper backing.

10. Position the shapes *adhesive side down*, around the block of lettering (See item 7). Readjust until a pleasing arrangement is achieved. Fuse everything in place as described earlier.

11. To finish, attach the lining and secure hems and casings as needed.

Free-form banners such as this one are not only a joy to produce, but they also often generate favorable responses. They work well during the long after-Pentecost summer months when variety is pleasant.

The Church Year

Advent

Ps. 43:3

Banner 2

Epiphany
John 8:12

Banner 4

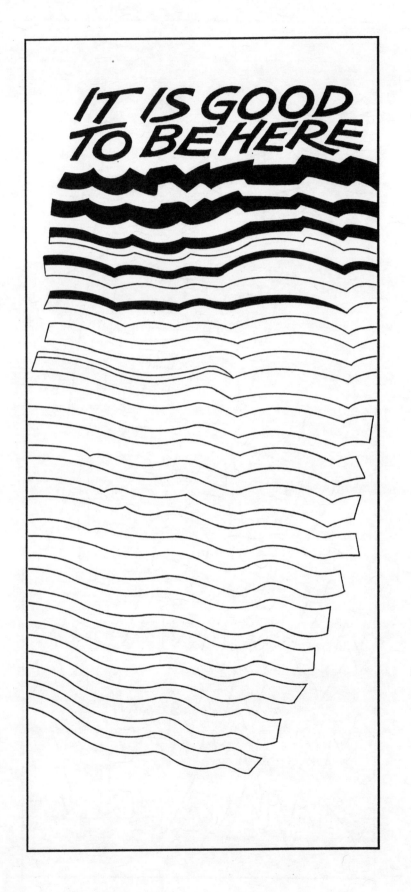

Lent
Ps. 22:11

Banner 6

Easter

Luke 24:33–34

Banner 8

After Pentecost I
Eph. 5:14

Banner 10

After Pentecost III

Ps. 46:1

Banner 12

The Christian Life
Baptism
LBW, p. 124

Banner 14

Eucharist
LW 247, LBW 221
....
Banner 15

Marriage
Gen. 12:2
....

Banner 16

Funeral
LW 509, LBW 448

Banner 18

A Time for . . .
Eccl. 3:1–8
Despair
Verse 6
....
Banner 19

Injury
Verse 3
. . . .

Banner 20

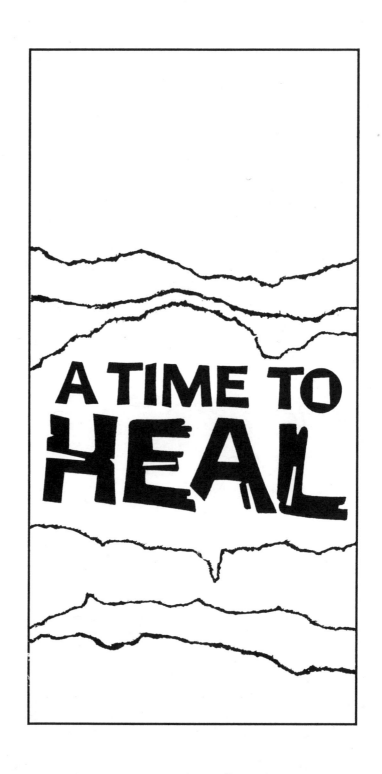

Chaos/Verse 8

Banner 22

Sadness/Verse 4

Banner 23

Prayers: Reflective
God's Will
Blaise Pascal

Banner 24

God's Peace
St. Francis of Assisi

Banner 25

God's People
Malcolm Boyd

Banner 27

GIVE US THE JOY OF SHARING OUR FAITH

God's Path
Ps. 119:105
. . . .
Banner 29

Reassurance
The Good Shepherd
Ps. 23

Banner 30

The Lilies of the Field
Matt. 6:28–30

Banner 31

The Doubting Disciple
John 20:27

Banner 33

Prayers: Joyous
Appreciate the Idea
Ludwig van Beethoven

Banner 34

Appreciate the World
C. F. Alexander

Banner 35

Appreciate the Eternal
LW 454

Banner 37

Appreciate the Word
LBW 516

Banner 39

(Re)Creation

Illumination
Gen. 1:3–5

Banner 40

Aetherization
Gen. 1:6–10

Banner 41

Cultivation
Gen. 1:11–13

Banner 42

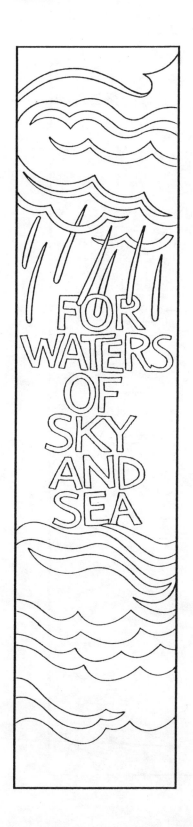

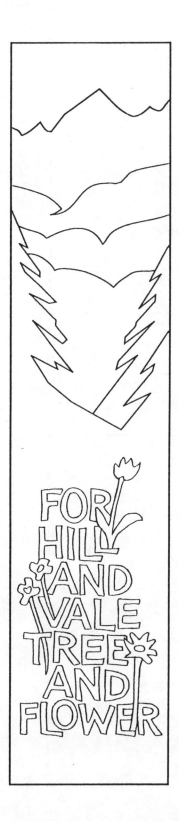

Synchronization
Gen. 1:14–19

Banner 43

Multiplication
Gen. 1:20–25

Banner 44

Population
Gen. 1:26–30

Banner 45

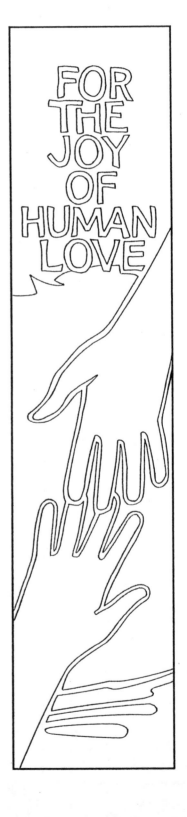

Evaluation/Gen. 1:31 ....

Banner 46

Revitalization/Rev. 21:5 ....

Banner 47

Processionals/LBW 509
Come and See/Ps. 46:8

Banner 48

Gloria
....

Banner 49

Banner 50

THINE
THE
GLORY

THINE
THE
PRAISE

He Lives

Banner 51

Stand Up

Banner 52

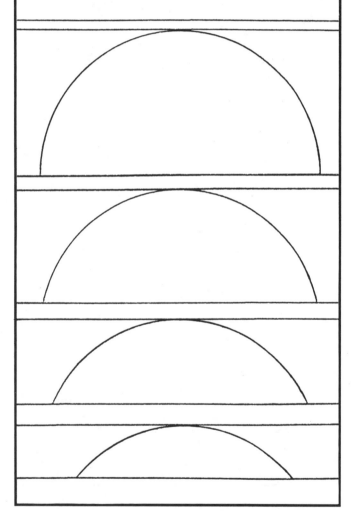

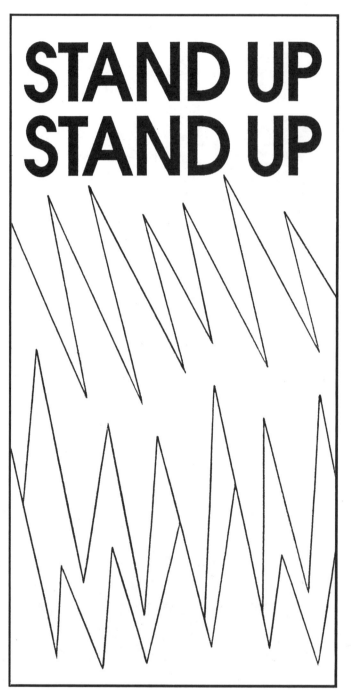

Fire

Banner 53

Joy

Banner 54

Rejoice

Banner 55

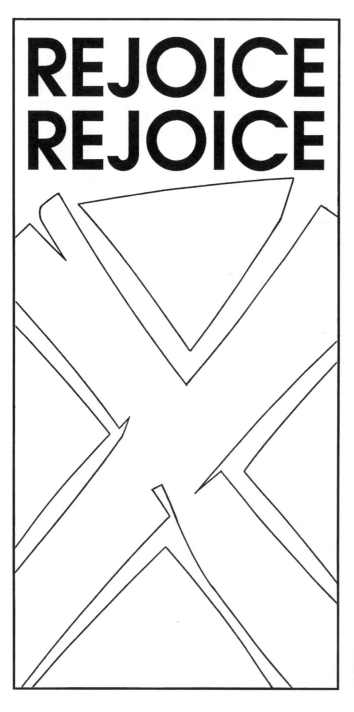

Enlightening Epistles
Communion/Eph. 2:13–19

Banner 57

Justification/Rom. 8:35

Banner 58

Love/1 Cor. 13:2

Banner 59

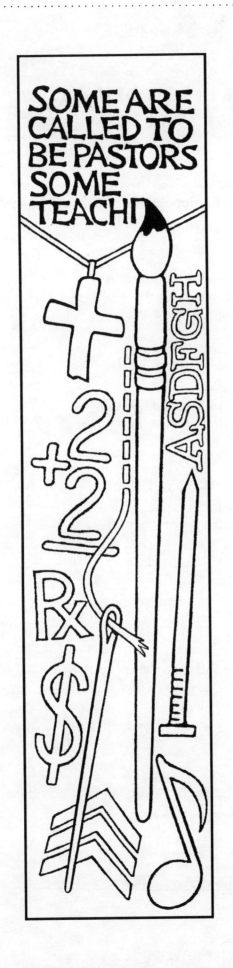

PART THREE

NOTES ON THE BANNER DESIGNS

The Church Year

This first group of designs makes a visual journey through the church year. Completion of all 12 banners yields a basic set highlighting each of the major festivals and seasons.

Advent/Ps. 43:3   Banner 2

The most important stage in developing a banner is the selection of the idea, belief, or central concept that the visual image is to express. The focus for this design was the Old Testament messianic prophecies:

"A star will come out of . . . Jacob" (Num. 24:17).

"I sit in darkness, the LORD will be my light" (Micah 7:8).

"Nations will come to your light" (Is. 60:3).

Light is the common link, and this led to Ps. 43:3: "Send forth your light and your truth, let them guide me" neatly embodies the theme of hope, faith, and light in the midst of darkness.

Make the lettering white (1).

Though the words dominate the design, the seemingly random shapes in the lower third of the banner are intended to intrigue. After a while, it becomes apparent that they define in negative space the familiar Christmas-Epiphany symbol, a five-point star.

Christmas/Ps. 66:5   Banner 3

Ps. 66:5 provides the words for this design: "Come and see what God has done, how awesome his works in man's behalf!"

Make the lettering and all the stars white (1).

The somewhat crude lettering is a deliberate contrast to the smooth lines of the hills and buildings. It is meant to give the design an added element of visual interest, so there is no need to make smooth cuts.

Epiphany/John 8:12   Banner 4

Two verses from John's gospel provided the inspiration here: "In him was life, and that life was the light of men"(John 1:4), and, "I am the light of the world. Whoever follows me will never walk in darkness, but will have the light of life" (John 8:12).

Make the lettering white (1).

Use the alternate version of the star to give this design a different

look. Copy it at 100% and substitute it for the other one and its shadow. For a true expression of light shattering the darkness, use fluorescent colors on a black background. (Choose one of the solid fluorescent shades of Lycra. It is somewhat expensive, and a fusible web will be needed for bonding, but the resulting effect is spectacular.)

Transfiguration/Matt. 17:4   Banner 5

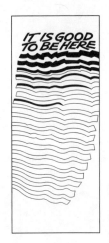

At the moment of the Transfiguration, Peter says, "It is good . . . to be here" (Matt. 17:4).

Rather than a literal illustration, three figures standing on a mountaintop, the focus here is on the light from God that reveals the promise of salvation as personified in Jesus Christ.

The colors progress from dark to light to create an illusion of movement. They also subtly allude to the one symbol consistently connected with covenant—the rainbow.

Make the lettering and all shapes shown in the drawing as black, white (1).

Lent/Ps. 22:11   Banner 6

The words come not from the Gospel narratives but from Ps. 22:11: "Do not be far from me, for trouble is near and there is no one to help." The abstract shapes surrounding the words foreshadow Jesus' Good Friday ordeal—hands and feet pierced by nails, thorns for a crown, searing-numbing pain, a sun retreating into hiding and an omnipresent cross.

Not a traditional Latin cross, this is a patriarchal cross. Its small upper arm recalls the inscription placed over Jesus' head by Pontius Pilate (John 19:19). This form was often used to identify church patriarchs and has come to represent great dedication in service to God and church.

Make the lettering white (1).

Palm Sunday/Gal. 2:19–20   Banner 7

The words are taken from Gal. 2:19–20, "For through the law I died to the law so that I might live for God. I have been crucified with Christ and I no longer live, but Christ lives in me."

Make the lettering white (1).

Note the two *TH* combinations, and how, with a little imagination, more lettering can be made to fit into narrow spaces without losing legibility or effect. It adds visual interest and forces the eye to see the letters in the same moment as conveyers of meaning and important design elements. (See also banners 10 and 13.)

This design was developed using a variation of the brainstorming process described on page 90. To give the shapes a graceful dancing motion, slightly thinned acrylic paint was applied with a 1/4" round brush in quick, calligraphy-like strokes on sheets of white paper. When dry, the painted shapes (palm branches, letters and cross) were cut out and arranged roughly on a sheet of black paper scaled to the proportion of the finished banner. The shapes were moved and trimmed until a satisfactory arrangement was achieved. Then they were attached with a glue stick. An opaque projector was used to enlarge the design to make a paper pattern. If you have access only to an overhead projector, mark an outline of the banner proportions on a clear acetate sheet and arrange the shapes on it. This will give you a "shadow" image to trace for the full-size paper pattern.

Easter/Luke 24:33–34   Banner 8

With a bold splash, the rising sun reveals an empty tomb. The story of the Resurrection was repeated many times in the following days.

Luke 24:33–34 provided the inspiration for this design: "They [Cleopas and his companion] got up and returned at once to Jerusalem. There they found the Eleven and those with them, assembled together and saying, 'It is true! The Lord has risen.' "

Make the lettering white (1).

For added visual interest, use yarn or embroidery paints to outline the pieces that make up the rising sun. For example, outline the white (1) with orange (9) or deep yellow (11); put a line of crimson red (5) along the edge of the old gold (10) shape, and a burgundy (4) along the edge of the mandarin orange (8) shape. Outlining, besides adding definition to the color area, covers any rough cuts or frayed edges, resulting in a more professional look.

Pentecost/Acts 2:1–4   Banner 9

This design is an invitation to the Holy Spirit to fire the lives of Christians and transform their reluctance into the courage and conviction needed to carry out their commission from God.

Make the lettering white (1).

If the alternate version of the dove is used, consider using black (2) for the background and fluorescent tones for the pink (7) and orange (9) design elements. To get a feel for this combination, copy the design from the book with a photocopier and color it appropriately with a black marker and fluorescent highlighting markers.

After Pentecost I/Eph. 5:14   Banner 10

This design came out of a study of Ephesians, which is particularly rich in picturesque themes. It is based on two passages in chapter 5: "You were once darkness, but now you are light in the Lord" (v. 8), and "Christ will shine on you" (v. 14). In the context of this banner, the witty synthesis of ideas becomes a prayer for God's continuing presence and interaction in the life of the individual Christian.

Make the lettering yellow (11).

After Pentecost II/Luke 15:23–24   Banner 11

The inspiration for this design was drawn from Jesus' parable of the lost son, Luke 15, and focuses on verses 23–24, "Let's have a feast and celebrate. For this son of mine was dead and is alive again." The father was so overjoyed, no matter what the circumstances of his son's return, that he wanted to throw a party and welcome him back. The father is an example of total, unconditional love.

There is nothing profoundly theological about the symbols for this banner. It is quite simply a visual party, with streamers, flowing ribbons, and confetti.

Make the lettering white (1).

After Pentecost III/Ps. 46:1   Banner 12

"God is our refuge and strength, an ever-present help in trouble" opens Psalm 46. Though only 11 verses long, it is packed with images expressing God's power and love.

The words are set within an ominous storm-laden sky, yet the flower survives, strong against the forces attempting to blow it over.

Make the lettering and the flower white (1).

Use templates to help in positioning the flower pieces:

After tracing the design onto paper, number everything and add corresponding numbers to the original design. While cutting the pieces out, save the discarded pieces to use as templates for final positioning. Then, as needed, tack them in place with a few pins. This extra step eliminates many problems, especially with curves that can become twisted easily.

After Pentecost IV/1 Thess. 5:16–18   Banner 13

"Give thanks with Joy" is a fitting exhortation for the end of the church year. The words are derived from the benediction that concludes 1 Thessalonians, "Be joyful always; pray continually; give thanks in all circumstances, for this is God's will for you in Christ Jesus" (5:16–18).

Make the lettering light blue (16).

It is not necessary to keep the lettering as a single block, especially if gluing. It is important with any cloth banner that design elements lay absolutely flat as they are bonded into position. One or two twisted lines can cause the banner to pucker or bulge, creating a problem with hanging.

With any intricate piece, it is a good idea to save the triangles, squares, rectangles, ovals, and irregular shapes left over from cutting the design elements. Then reassemble everything, the letters, the rest of the design, and the discards (that otherwise would go into the fabric scrap bin) on the background as if they were all pieces of a giant jigsaw puzzle. Pick up each design element individually in turn for gluing. The temporarily placed negative cuts will make it clear where things go as they are put back into place permanently..

The Christian Life

The next five designs highlight the important times and events in a Christian's life, from Baptism to death. All are in a square format.

Baptism/*LBW*, p. 124   Banner 14

With every Baptism comes a reminder of the Christian's status as an adopted child of God. Even when not in use, the baptismal font is a silent yet constant reminder of the promise of eternal life. In this context, banners can be very effective, whether hung on the wall behind the font or suspended on a pole nearby.

To emphasize the underlying concept of rebirth, the colors suggested for this banner are those of the sunrise normally associated with Easter.

Before beginning, decide if the lower part of the lettering block (indicated in the outline) is to be solid white or turned into a rainbow using the painting technique described earlier in "Learning Useful Techniques."

Eucharist/*LW* 247, *LBW* 221   Banner 15

The words for this design are taken from stanza 2 of *Sent Forth by God's Blessing*, "With your feast you feed us, / With your light now lead us; / Unite us as one in this life that we share." They are a reminder that Holy Communion is a family as well as a sacramental meal. Bread is broken, wine is poured, the words are said: "The body of Christ broken . . . the blood of Christ shed . . . " Together the congregation partakes of the past, present, and future feast.

Make the lettering magenta (21).

Once everything has been bonded, the bread or "hosts" may need a subtle outline of either white (1) or ginger (22) yarn to give the banner a finished look.

Marriage/Gen. 12:2   Banner 16

Good wedding banners are difficult to design. This one goes back to Gen.12:2 and part of God's sevenfold covenant with Abram—"I will bless you; I will make your name great, and you will be a blessing"—for its slogan. The thoughtful message on the banner is appropriate because each marriage is a reaffirmation of that original covenant.

The words are tied together with flowing interwoven ribbons to express unity and movement.

The top area is left open to allow the design to be individualized by adding a Bible verse, hymn line, or the names of the bride and groom. Use one of the quick lettering techniques described in "Learning Useful Techniques," or purchase vinyl lettering sets (3" or 4") from an office supply or art store.

This banner can also be made into a permanent personal keepsake by using the colors of the birthstones of the bride and groom, one for the background, the other for the ribbons.

Celebration/Ps. 149:1–3   Banner 17

"Sing to the LORD a new song, . . . Let Israel rejoice in their Maker. . . . Let them praise his name with dancing" (Ps. 149:1–3). With its ribbons and balloons, this multipurpose design would well serve a confirmation, an anniversary, or a wedding. It is also appropriate for a funeral in that it celebrates life, and a better life just beginning.

For the words, make sing *yellow (11), dance old gold (10), and* rejoice *pink (7). Though magenta (21) is designated for the background, royal blue (19), violet (20), or forest green (14) would also work. The deciding factor might be the color scheme of the area where this banner is to be displayed.*

The bottom of the design is intentionally left open.

The list of confirmands, the names of the couple, or a favorite Bible verse may be added. As with wedding banner 16, purchased, self-adhesive vinyl lettering sets can be used. If, on the other hand, letters from one of the quick-lettering patterns are used, they may be attached with double-stick tape. This technique allows the letters to be used for a specific occasion, removed, and saved for reuse later.

It is also possible, even desirable, to leave the design just as it is. The empty space can be seen as a support for and a contrast to the activity at the top. Here is a good example of one negative that is also a positive.

Funeral/*LW* 509, *LBW* 448   Banner 18

Banners are not usually a priority when planning funerals. Keep in mind that the floral tributes, specially chosen music, and remembrances from family and friends do not help the dead. They are offered to facilitate the grieving process of the living. If a special funeral banner is already on hand, it too can be used as a means of comfort.

The words for this banner come from stanza 3 of *Amazing Grace*, "Through many dangers, toils, and snares / I have already come; / 'Tis grace has brought me safe thus far, / And grace will lead me home" (*LBW* 448, *LW* 509).

Make the lettering black (2).

A Time for . . . /Eccl. 3:1–8

This series was inspired by Eccl. 3:1, "There is a time for everything, and a season for every activity under heaven."

These five designs can be used individually or as a set to highlight special events or worship themes. They could provide a springboard for a collaboration with the pastor or worship committee in developing a series of Advent meditations.

The artistic goal for the series was to achieve a simplicity of design appropriate to the simplicity of the messages.

Despair/Verse 6   Banner 19

" . . . a time to search and a time to give up,
a time to keep and a time to throw away."

If constructing the complete set, begin with this design. Trace the letters of the words a time for onto cardstock (a file folder, for instance) to use as stencils, as they are repeated throughout the series.

For this banner, make the lettering white (1).

Injury/Verse 3   Banner 20

" . . . a time to kill and a time to heal,
a time to tear down and a time to build."

Note the rough edges. Either rip the cloth in short bursts, or make jagged cuts; there is no need to be precise. Be spontaneous. Then use a black permanent marker along the edges to emphasize their rough quality.

Make the lettering gray (3).

Anticipation/Verse 5   Banner 21

" . . . a time to scatter stones and a time to gather them,
a time to embrace and a time to refrain."

This is a scene of winter, with trees standing stark against a gray landscape, the few remaining leaves losing their grip to a cold north wind. The image is one of desolation, but the knowledgeable can see the promise of renewal hidden within the presently dormant earth.

Make the blowing leaves yellow (11) and the lettering gray (3). Outline the trees and blowing leaves with a black permanent marker. Use a thin line around the leaves. a thicker (1/8"–3/16") one for the trees, as indicated by the illustration.

Chaos/Verse 8   Banner 22

" . . . a time to love and a time to hate,
a time for war and a time for peace."

Peace is the opposite of chaos, noise, and violence. The slogan in the center of this design is a cry for at least a momentary respite from the seemingly uncontrollable pace of everyday life.

Make the lettering white (1).

Sadness/Verse 4   Banner 23

" . . . a time to weep and a time to laugh,
a time to mourn and a time to dance."

One of the greatest musical expressions of joy is found in Beethoven's *Ninth Symphony.* The "Ode to Joy" opens with praise, "Joyful, joyful we adore thee, God of glory, Lord of love," and concludes with a prayer, "Teach us how to love each other, Lift us to the joy divine!"

With music in mind, the composition of this banner suggests the longed for upward movement into that great, glorious, inexpressible state.

Make the lettering white (1).

Prayers: Reflective

"Do not be anxious about anything, but in everything, by prayer and petition, with thanksgiving, present your requests to God" (Phil. 4:6).

"And when you pray, do not keep on babbling like pagans, for they think they will be heard because of their many words" (Matt. 6:7).

Banners can be thought of as prayers in visual form. They can offer, for instance, petition, intercession, confession, praise, or thanksgiving. They also follow Jesus' recommended style—to be brief and to the point.

The designs in this series are petitions for guidance and assistance in living a responsible Christian life.

God's Will/Blaise Pascal   Banner 24

"O Lord, let me not henceforth desire health or life, except to spend them for you. . . . You alone know what is good for me; do, therefore, what seems best to you. . . . Conform my will to yours"— from a prayer by French mathematician and religious philosopher Blaise Pascal (1623–62).

This thought recalls Ps. 143:10: "Teach me to do your will, for you are my God"; and even more so Jesus' prayer in Gethsemane: "Yet not what I will, but what you will" (Mark 14:36).

Make the lettering white (1).

God's Peace/St. Francis of Assisi   Banner 25

"Lord, make me an instrument of your peace. Where there is hatred, let me sow love; where there is injury, pardon; where there is doubt, faith; where there is despair, hope; where there is darkness, light; where there is sadness, joy"—prayer attributed to St. Francis of Assisi (1182–1226), founder of the Franciscan Order.

Make the lettering white (1).

God's Service/St. Ignatius Loyola   Banner 26

"Teach us, Good Lord, to serve you as you deserve: To give and not to count the cost; To fight and not to heed the wounds; To toil and not to seek for rest; To labor and not to ask for any reward save that of knowing that we do your will"—prayer for generosity of St. Ignatius Loyola (1491–1556), founder of the Jesuits.

Make the lettering old gold (10).

For the coins, use a fabric with a simulated metallic finish, such as tissue lamé. Solid colors in gold, silver, and copper are best. The results will be excellent but the fabric requires special treatment.

Since this material shreds easily and does not accept glue well, apply fusible web before cutting the shapes. Use a fusible web specifically made for lightweight fabrics to prevent the adhesive from seeping through onto the surface of this rather filmy and porous material.

Tissue lamé is also heat sensitive. Care should be taken not to place a hot iron directly on it. Check the fabric care instructions that come with it, and be sure always to cover it with a damp pressing cloth when ironing it.

God's People/Malcolm Boyd   Banner 27

"Help us to see persons, Jesus—not a black person or a white person, a red person or a yellow person, but human persons"—prayer by Episcopal priest Malcolm Boyd (b. 1923) from *Are You Running with Me, Jesus?*

For this banner it is possible to use the colors of the human palette, red, black, yellow, brown, and white. To carry the idea effectively, however, use instead the neutrals of gray, green, and blue, with only enough white to define the shapes and give them life. Or, instead of the green and blue solids, consider using a multicolored floral or bold geometric print.

God's Gift/Roy Gesch   Banner 28

"Give us the joy of sharing our faith with each other that we can be one in worship and prayer at home and at church"—prayer by Lutheran pastor Roy Gesch (b. 1920) from *A Husband Prays*.

The design juxtaposes hearts filled with Christ and hearts incomplete or void. It would be appropriate any time, but especially during the Pentecost season or whenever the focus is on evangelism.

Make the lettering white (1).

God's Path/Ps. 119:105   Banner 29

"Your word is a lamp to my feet and a light for my path" (Ps. 119:105).

This design is adapted easily for other purposes. The symbolism of the path lends itself well to use as an overall theme for Advent. One of the designated texts for Advent, for instance, is Matt. 3:3. Complete the banner as shown but substitute "Prepare the way for the Lord," or "Make straight paths for him."

Banners without words are often just as effective in conveying a theme. There is, for instance, a striking image in stanza 3 of "Hail to the Lord's Anointed (*LW* 82, *LBW* 87), "He shall come down like showers/Upon the fruitful earth;/And love, joy, hope, like flowers,/Spring in his path to birth."

Take your box of saved fabric scraps. Cut simple flowers (daisies, tulips, sunflowers, etc.) to fill the path with a brightly colored mixture. Start with larger ones at the bottom and make them gradually smaller toward the top.

Reassurance

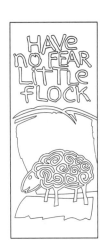

The next four designs have the general theme of comfort and assurance.

The Good Shepherd/Psalm 23   Banner 30

There is perhaps no more comforting image found in the Bible than that of the Good Shepherd guarding his flock or searching for the 1 lamb separated from the other 99. It has provided spiritual sustenance during times of trial and persecution since the earliest years of Christianity.

This banner was designed specifically for Good Shepherd Sunday. Logical hymns to go with this theme might include "The King of Love My Shepherd Is" (*LW* 412, *LBW* 456, *TLH* 431) and "The Lord's My Shepherd" (*LW* 416, *LBW* 451, *TLH* 436). But "Have No Fear Little Flock" (*LW* 410, *LBW* 476) expresses the very precise feeling of childlike trust.

Actually the patterns for the words and animal were done by a little girl. With a crayon, she produced crude lettering and a puff-ball of a lamb with stick legs. Her drawing was then photocopied and enlarged to full banner size with an opaque projector, thus capturing much of her original directness and innocence.

When cutting out the letters, keep the lines crude and unrefined, carrying the qualities of the original crayon over to the banner.

All the lines and swirls making up the "lamb" are white (1).

The Lilies of the Field/Matt. 6:28–30   Banner 31

"And why do you worry about clothes? See how the lilies of the field grow. They do not labor or spin. Yet I tell you that not even Solomon in all his splendor was dressed like one of these. If that is how God clothes the grass of the field, which is here today and tomorrow is thrown into the fire, will he not much more clothe you?" (Matt. 6:28–30).

Make the lettering fuchsia (6).

If desired, it is possible to give this design added depth. Take a set of washable (not permanent) markers and lightly sketch a 1/2"–3/4" wide line around the centers (stamens) of each of the flowers. Use a color in the same range as the color of the cloth for the petals, but darker (e.g., red on pink, dark blue on medium blue, orange on yellow). Then, with a 1/2" wide brush, lightly brush the marker-colored area and a little more with plain tap water. This will cause the marker to bleed and become softer and watercolorlike.

The Lost Child   Banner 32

The focus of this banner is on the concluding words of the parable of the lost son (Luke 15:11–32), "This brother of yours was dead and is alive again; he was lost and is found." The theme is repeated in

personal terms in the familiar opening stanza of "Amazing Grace"
(*LW* 509, *LBW* 448), "Amazing grace, / How sweet the sound, / That
saved a wretch like me! / I once was lost, but now am found; / Was
blind, but now I see."

Make the lettering royal blue (19).

Or change the color scheme and the meaning of the design with
it. Depending on the colors used, the jagged lines emanating from the
top could represent: (1) the reverberation of the sweet sound of
grace, (2) the radiance of the light that cures spiritual blindness, (3)
the shattering of the barrier between lost and found, or (4) the earth-
shaking quality of the salvation experience.

The Doubting Disciple/John 20:27   Banner 33

John 20:24–27 encapsulates the earthly answer Jesus provides
for Thomas' earthly question: "[Thomas] said to [the other disciples],
'Unless I see the nail marks in his hands and put my finger where the
nails were, and put my hand into his side, I will not believe it.' . . .
Then [Jesus] said to Thomas, 'Put your finger here; see my hands.
Reach out your hand and put it into my side. Stop doubting and
believe.' "

The design of this banner is intended to be just as bold and
straightforward as Jesus was with Thomas. Look at the hand pierced
through by the nail, and be blessed as a believer.

Make the lettering crimson red (5).

Prayers: Joyous
. . . .

Following is another series of visual prayers, this one joyous
hymns of praise.

Appreciate the Idea/Ludwig van Beethoven   Banner 34

The words for this design come from a prayer by Ludwig van
Beethoven (1770–1827): "O lead my spirit, O raise it from these
weary depths that, ravished by your art, it may strive upwards with
tempestuous fire. For you alone have knowledge, you alone can
inspire enthusiasm."

To best understand the image, try to see the design elements as
the swirls and strokes of a large paint brush.

Make the lettering white (1).

the others. First display one, then add a second, and a third, and so on, until after seven weeks all the banners hang together to create one unified message. Leave them up for a few weeks, then take them down, and pack them away for another time. If left up too long banners tend, like the pews and windows, to become fixtures, and people start taking them for granted.

Illumination/Gen. 1:3–5 Banner 40

"And God said, 'Let there be light' " (Gen. 1:3).

Aetherization/Gen. 1:6–10 Banner 41

"And God said, 'Let there be an expanse between the waters to separate water from water' " (Gen. 1:6).

Cultivation/Gen. 1:11–13 Banner 42

"Then God said, 'Let the land produce vegetation' " (Gen. 1:11).

Synchronization/Gen. 1:14–19 Banner 43

"And God said, 'Let there be lights in the expanse of the sky to separate the day from the night, and let them serve as signs to mark seasons and days and years' " (Gen. 1:14).

Multiplication/Gen. 1:20–25 Banner 44

"And God said, 'Let the water teem with living creatures, and let birds fly above the earth across the expanse of the sky. . . . Let the land produce living creatures according to their kinds' " (Gen. 1:20–24).

The eyes of all the creatures are chestnut (23).

The elephant's ear can be defined either by using a black permanent marker or an overlay piece of self (gray) fabric.

Population/Gen. 1:26–30 Banner 45

"Then God said, 'Let us make man in our image' " (Gen. 1:26).

Evaluation/Gen. 1:31 Banner 46

"God saw all that he had made, and it was very good" (Gen. 1:31).

Revitalization/Rev. 21:5 Banner 47

From alpha to omega, God is consistent. At the end of the book, as at the beginning, "He who was seated on the throne said, 'I am making everything new!' " (Rev. 21:5).

Try making this design out of white linen. The cross-hatched lines represent roughly cut pieces of natural burlap (the looser the weave, the better) mixed with scraps of unbleached muslin. To emphasize the crude-

ness, add a couple of rough holes and a patch or two. Incorporate, if available, an old stained piece of cloth ripped into shreds. Choose either a royal blue (19), mandarin orange (8), or crimson red (5) for the letters.

Processionals

"Onward, Christian soldiers, marching as to war, /With the cross of Jesus / Going on before. Christ the royal master, / Leads against the foe; / Forward into battle / See, his banners go!" (*LW* 518, *LBW* 509, *TLH* 658).

Processional banners are among the oldest traditions of the church. In the 6th century, *Vexilla* (crosses with red streamers attached), were used for street processions in Rome. Although processional banners seem to have fallen out of favor, they can still play a roll in worship as visual rallying cries. They add an element of movement that stationary hangings cannot provide. They are most appropriate when worshiping in an outdoor setting (e.g., at a retreat) or when services begin outside the sanctuary (e.g., on Palm Sunday, or at an Easter sunrise service).

Processional banners should not be too large; the size and age of the bearers (most likely 10- to 14-year-olds) need to be kept in mind when designing them. A good size is about 30" × 60"; the maximum recommended size is about 3' × 6'. The carrying pole is also a concern. The banner should not swing back and forth or flop around as can happen with cords. Using a T-shaped pole eliminates these problems. (See the section "Display" earlier in this book.) It also needs to be remembered that processional banners have both a back and a front, and that both sides are seen about the same length of time. For this reason, they need to be lined, preferably with the same material as that used for the background of the front design.

All the designs in this series have the same classic 2-to-1 proportions and lettering style. The computer-generated font *Avant Garde* has only straight lines and circles, and thus the only tools required for tracing the letters are a rule and a compass.

Come and See/Ps. 46:8   Banner 48

This general-use design is based on Ps. 46:8: "Come and see the works of the LORD." It contains a Greek cross, that is, a cross with arms of equal length, done in a southwestern style.

The design utilizes all of the liturgical colors— white (1), black (2), red (5), yellow (11), green (14), blue (19), violet (20). It is appropriate for any time of the year, but especially Christmas, Christ the King Sunday, and Easter.

Gloria   Banner 49

The text for this design was adapted from "Thine Is the Glory" (*LBW* 145). Its tone suits a time of celebration.

Make the lettering white (1).

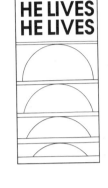

Praise/John 12:12–13   Banner 50

This design is especially good for Palm Sunday. Its concept is drawn from John 12:12–13, " The next day the great crowd that had come for the Feast heard that Jesus was on his way to Jerusalem. They took palm branches and went out to meet him, shouting, 'Hosanna!' "

Make the lettering white (1).

He Lives/*LW* 264   Banner 51

This banner was specifically designed with Easter in mind. The words are taken from "I Know that My Redeemer Lives" (*LW* 264, *LBW* 352, *TLH* 200): "I know that my Redeemer lives! / What comfort this sweet sentence gives! / He lives, he lives, who once was dead; / He lives, my ever-living head!"

Make the lettering black (2).

Stand Up   Banner 52

Here is a rallying cry for witness. The words come from "Stand Up, Stand Up for Jesus" (*LW* 305, *LBW* 389, *TLH* 451): "Stand up, stand up for Jesus / As soldiers of the cross. / Lift high his royal banner . . . "

Make the lettering white (1).

Fire   Banner 53

Make this banner for Pentecost. It was inspired by the words of "Come, Oh, Come, O Quickening Spirit" (*LW* 165, *LBW* 478, *TLH* 226): "God before the dawn of time! / Fire our hearts with holy ardor."

Make the lettering white (1).

Joy   Banner 54

This banner is appropriate for the Epiphany or Pentecost season and for music services. The slogan was inspired by the refrain from "For the Beauty of the Earth" (*LBW* 561): "Christ, our Lord, to you we raise / this our sacrifice of praise."

Make the lettering black (2).

Rejoice   Banner 55

From a hymn appointed for Christmas, "Rejoice, Rejoice This Happy Morn" (*LW* 520, *LBW* 43, *TLH* 79), come the words, "Rejoice, rejoice this happy morn, / A Savior unto us is born." The St. Andrew's cross is a reminder of the reason for Jesus' birth.

Make the lettering black (2).

For a change, replace the cross with an adaptation of a flower from another one of the designs in this book. See the funeral design (banner 18) or the hope design (banner 19). It would then become a good Advent banner, recalling the rose of Sharon, the messianic rose in Song of Songs 2:1, and the hymn "Lo, How a Rose Is Growing" (*LW* 67, *LBW* 58, *TLH* 645). Use pink for the flower, green for the stem, white for the letterings, and place everything on a dark blue background.

Be Glad/M. K. Blanchard   Banner 56

For the Easter or Pentecost seasons, this design is based on the song "Be Ye Glad!" by Michael Kelly Blanchard. It contains the words "Every debt has been paid in full by the grace of the Lord. Be ye glad! Be ye glad!"

Make the lettering black (2).

Enlightening Epistles

The last series highlights themes from Paul's letters.

Communion/Eph. 2:13–19   Banner 57

This design depicts the essence of what Paul states in Eph. 2:13–19: "In Christ Jesus you who once were far away have been brought near through the blood of Christ. . . . you are no longer foreigners and aliens, but fellow citizens with God's people and members of God's household."

To convey the concept of oneness in Christ, the cross is made of many interwoven parts, each individually frail, but strong as a part of the larger whole. "In him the whole . . . is joined together" (Eph. 2:21).

Make the lettering white (1).

The strips making up the cross are one color—pink (7). Two alternating colors, pink and blue, were tested but they made the cross look disjointed and not the symbol of unity needed here.

Justification/Rom. 8:35   Banner 58

Literally, Rom. 8:35 asks a question: "Who shall separate us from the love of Christ?" Here it is an affirmation of faith. The word *separate* may be physically divided on the banner, but *we* are not separated from the *love of God.*

Make the lettering white (1).

Love/1 Cor. 13:2   Banner 59

Paul writes in 1 Cor. 13:2, "If I have a faith that can move mountains, but have not love, I am nothing."

Outline the jagged shape around the words "is nothing without love" with orange (9) to match that on the lower part of "faith."

Grace/Eph. 4:11–12   Banner 60

"It was he who gave some to be apostles, some to be prophets, some to be evangelists, and some to be pastors and teachers, to prepare God's people for works of service, so that the body of Christ may be built up" (Eph. 4:11–12).

This banner amplifies Paul's statement that everyone's abilities are not only gifts from God but can be used to build up the body of

Christ. Instead of spelling out various professions (artist, banker, carpenter, musician, pharmacist, soldier, tailor), symbols have been used for them. Vary the design of the banner by highlighting different professions.

To simplify construction, pick a deep blue, red, or green for the background. Make the symbols white (1) and either glue or fuse them in place. The brush tip should be the same color as the slogan it is being used to write, here, pink (7). With a black medium-tip permanent marker, outline each one of the symbols and draw in all of the details.

DESIGN IDEAS: THEMES AND VARIATIONS

SELF-DESIGN

Brainstorming Method

The best way to get creative juices flowing and thus come up with a great idea for a banner design is to utilize the process of brainstorming, otherwise known as thumbnailing. With notebook or sketch pad in hand, quickly sketch out lots of ideas as fast as possible no matter how radical or improbable. Remember, nothing is more limiting than *one* idea. Thumbnails, as the term implies, should be small (about 2" square) so they all fit on one or two pages. When there are at least 10 ideas, sift them and begin eliminating ideas until only 2 or 3 are left. Enlarge and polish these, refining graphic forms and lines and sorting through possible colors. Next, pick the best one of these, turn it into a line drawing (like the ones in this book), and copy it onto an overhead projection transparency. It is now possible to transform that idea into a physical reality.

A key component of the creative process is flexibility. The mind needs to be kept open to possibilities. As work proceeds, continue to question, explore, and adapt. Would an element work better in a different color? Would a rough or smooth texture accent a particular area? Does the addition of this shape upset the overall design? Is the slogan too long? These are just a few of the questions that might be asked and, if the answer to any is yes, acted upon.

Spontaneous Method

Another, more immediate, way to create a design is to use the spontaneous approach.

Materials

- Background cloth (felt is a good choice because it does not require lining) in a favorite color, and in a size and proportion to fit the display area. Make necessary hem allowances for hanging.

- 1/2' each of three or four different colors of a mostly cotton fabric for the design pieces (try broadcloth or poly-cotton sheeting). Coordinate these colors with each other and the background, being sure they work together well.

- Fusible web, for bonding. Purchase enough material to totally cover the cloth for the design pieces.

- Sharp scissors.

- Iron and pressing cloth.

Procedure

1. Place the background on the floor so it can be looked at from a distance and from different perspectives.

2. Bond the fusible adhesive to the back of the fabric for the design elements, following the directions furnished with the material.

3. If the word theme has not been chosen, open the Bible to the Psalms, or a hymnal anywhere, and begin reading through the verses or stanzas and, without analyzing them, jotting down any phrases that strike a responsive chord. Do not stop with one.

4. Begin sifting through the choices, tossing out the inappropriate ones or even rewriting them until there is one phrase left that suits the banner. With a large marker, write it down as a reminder while work proceeds.

5. With scissors in hand, begin cutting out the letters. Use a variety of colors or just one. Try cutting directly without relying on pencil guidelines. When finished, peel off the paper backing and place it loosely on the background *cloth side up*. This will give a good idea of how much space there is to work with.

6. Next, cut out a variety of silhouette shapes in different colors. They can be geometric (squares, circles, triangles), linear (curves, zigzags, straight orthogonals), organic (animals, heavenly bodies, plants). Let the chosen phrase suggest ideas. Try not to use predrawn guidelines. This may seem difficult at first, but it is possible to *feel* the shapes and actually draw with the scissors. As the shapes are cut, peel off the paper backing and place them on the background with the letters. Often just the process of doing a preliminary arrangement will suggest possibilities for other shapes.

7. Spaces are either positive or negative. Positive space is the shape itself. Negative space is the empty area around the shape, and it is as important to any design as the positive space. Keep this in mind as you move the shapes and letters around the background, looking for a pleasing arrangement. Not all the negative space needs to be filled. Watch the negative spaces change as the shapes are moved to new positions. Also, instead of lumping the lines of letters into a single block, split them and work the shapes in between. This is the time to learn and experiment, because nothing is fastened permanently. For a change of perspective, stand up, walk around, and look at everything from the top or sides.

8. Finalize the arrangement. Be sure the letters are properly spaced. Preheat the iron. Follow the instructions with the fusible web for bonding. Add hems to the top and bottom and hang.

Finding a Niche

No matter how a banner is conceived and finally executed, it is important always to keep its ultimate purpose in mind. Banners are designed to play an important part in worship, and they do that best when they are well placed.

Banners are frequently displayed in the vicinity of the altar, table, or podium. But not all worship-related activities take place directly to the front. When worshipers turn to observe the choir, are their eyes confronted by an expanse of blank wall? As guests and members leave a meaningful worship experience, does the narthex or hallway outside the sanctuary serve only as egress to the parking lot? These are only two of the areas that bannermakers can utilize to subtly extend the worship experience or to invite people to participate in other church activities.

Remember, banners are not sales tools, like newspaper ads, nor are they propaganda, like posters. They are meant to excite, provoke thought, and create an atmosphere conducive to worship. Part of what makes banners interesting is that once they are put on display, they take on a life of their own. People not only see them, they experience them, and, depending upon their personal outlooks, draw different things from them.

A Word on Color

Early in the Bible, color was connected with meaningful worship. Beginning in Ex. 26:1, God, through Moses, instructs the Israelites to "make the tabernacle with ten curtains of finely twisted linen and blue, purple and scarlet yarn . . . "

The early church apparently used white throughout the year. Color to differentiate the seasons appeared gradually between the 9th and 13th centuries. It was not until the 16th century, however, that the church established the now familiar sequence of red, green, violet, black, and white. By virtue of their inherent moods and characteristics, these colors have subtly influenced worship for many decades.

Red (5), for example, is the warm color of life-giving blood. It is passion, love, caring, and sentimentality, but it can also be anger, sublimation, and war. Of all the colors of worship, it is the most powerful. A large splash of red demands attention. In liturgy, the church reserves red to commemorate Pentecost, Reformation, Palm Sunday, ordinations, and the days of various saints. These festivals, representing high emotion and God's call to action, like the color, cannot be ignored.

Green (14), the church's non-festival color, designates the two transitional periods known on the church calendar as "after the Epiphany" and "after Pentecost." Labeling them as such seems to imply that these periods are routine and unexciting. It is rather better to think of them as times of learning and growth in faith, times that challenge artists to find different and exciting ways to lend visual emphasis to the rich variety of messages from Jesus' ministry. Here, the vibrancy of the greens chosen is very important. These seasons call for the deep natural shades of summer leaves and grass.

The western world associates **black (2)** with mourning, absence, darkness, and death. Therefore, the church uses it only once, for the day of supreme seriousness, Good Friday. For bannermakers, however, it is an excellent background color. Virtually all other colors seem to advance, to pop out, when placed against it. Use black with restraint, because, as such a strong color, its effect can be overwhelming.

White (1) is the festival color of the church. In liturgy, it is reserved for celebrations that reflect themes of purity, light, innocence, holiness, and redemption, including Jesus' birth, baptism, transfiguration, and resurrection; Maundy Thursday and Thanksgiving. For the bannermaker it presents challenges. Although it is easy to use for letters and other design elements, as a background it can be intimidating. It tends to dominate, forcing boldness in the choice of colors and graphics. Timidity in the presence of white only results in design elements that get lost.

Violet (20) is most often associated with the Lenten season. As a combination of warm red (passion) and cool blue (calm), neither moving nor still, violet perfectly represents this most necessary season that refocuses from Jesus' hopeful birth to his agonizing death. Violet is preferable to purple for Lent, because purple suggests the pagan Roman imperium. Violet gives a truer portrayal of Lent's themes of humility, penitence, sorrow, and grief.

Blue (19) best represents the other season of thoughtful preparation, Advent. It gives Advent its own identity. In a worship setting, blue creates an atmosphere akin to that of darkness becoming light, of a new day dawning, filled with possibilities. And, like black, it is very accommodating; it works well with virtually any color. There is no better color to signify the beginning of the church year.

The nonliturgical color **yellow (11)** endows the worship environment with the glow and warmth of the sun. Used for Easter, it generates thoughts of the enlightening revelation of Jesus' empty tomb that vanquishes death and despair forever.

Throughout the church year, the varying colors used in worship unfold as a rainbow, affirming the constant presence of God's grace in the life of the individual Christian. Like Joseph's many-colored coat, the colors signify the believer as God's firstborn and heir to his promise of eternal life.